GENEALOGY

GENEALOGY

A BIBLE READING GUIDE

PETER LEBLANC

authorHOUSE®

AuthorHouse™
1663 Liberty Drive
Bloomington, IN 47403
www.authorhouse.com
Phone: 1-800-839-8640

Published by AuthorHouse   11/27/2012

ISBN: 978-1-4772-5720-3 (sc)

Introduction

Are we all one family? Does the Bible make sense? Who are all the people in the Bible? Is it believable or make believe? Is God accessible? Does God have a plan for creation? Does this plan include me? Who was Jesus? Why did he have to die? Is the Bible relevant to modern life? How can contemporary issues be addressed by documents that are 2000 years old or older? Can I learn from the experiences of the characters of the Bible?

These kinds of questions and others limit even the interested reader of the Bible. It may seem overwhelming to try to answer all these questions and the Bible may in fact be the last place people turn to try to find meaning. This should not be so since the Bible is full of amazing stories of people who tried to find answers to these questions and other more difficult questions.

This compilation of the Biblical genealogy is meant to encourage novices and long time readers to closely examine the stories and characters in the Bible. This book is designed to complement, rather than hinder the process of reading the Scriptures. A read through the Bible, complemented by this document will encourage a pattern of reading and studying the Bible. An excellent pattern would be to read through the Bible yearly. For help one can turn to a complementary book such as those listed in the references as an accompaniment to an annual read through the Bible.

All the thoughts in this book can be verified, tested or disputed by picking up a copy of the Bible and reading and testing what is contained here. The version of the Bible that was used here was the New American Standard Bible Reference Edition published by Moody Press. Almost any modern translation would work as a complement to this reading guide with perhaps some slight modifications in the spellings of names.

The Bible is a classic work of literature studied and read since before the time of the great Greek and Persian empires. The Old Testament was originally written in Hebrew and the New Testament was written in Greek. Since the Bible has long been studied, it has been divided into chapters and verses to ease the referencing and to make it easier to find portions that are cited. For example the book of Genesis has 50 chapters; each chapter has many verses.

There is a certain mystery and beauty about the Bible since it is a rich work of literature. Some of the mysteries contained in the Bible are hard to understand and make it seem as if we are seeing things through a veil. The Apostle Paul wrote on this point in a letter to the Corinthians, this passage is from the thirteenth chapter of the book of 1 Corinthians (Cor), also stated as 1 Cor. chapter 13 verses 9 through 12. It can also be written shorthand as 1 Cor 13:9-12:

> For we know in part and we prophesy in part;
> but when the perfect comes, the partial will be done away.
> When I was a child, I used to speak like a child, think like a child, reason like a child; when I became a man, I did away with childish things.
> For now we see in a mirror dimly, but then face to face; now I know in part, but then I will know fully just as I also have been fully known.
> This is an excerpt taken from the New American Standard Bible® (NASB).

This passage highlights the fact that what we know now is not what we will fully know. Additionally there is a wonder in store since the part we have will one day reach a fullness yet to be seen. We can read expectantly and trust that we will be guided into all truth (John 16:13).

There are also secret things that have not been revealed, as recorded in the book of Deuteronomy, chapter 29 in the first part of verse 29, "The secret things belong to the LORD our God," (NASB). In this space we have to admit we do not have all the information, we do not have a full perspective. We respect this space but there are many other things in the Bible that are not hidden. The things that have been revealed require a closer examination. The second part of

Deuteronomy 29:29 says this, "but the things revealed belong to us and to our sons forever, that we may observe all the words of this law" (NASB).

From these two passages discussed above we can see that some questions we ponder are good enough to command our attention for a life time. The Bible is a document worthy of reading and studying in detail, this is why most folks do not read the Bible just once. Although some material requires intense study, the Bible is accessible and some parts are easy to understand, these are sections that give clear answers. These clear things are clear directions, they are things worthy of our application and they answer our questions fully. So we cannot truthfully wave a hand at the Scripture and say that it is all mysterious and claim it is unknowable.

This presentation of the biblical genealogy will not nail down all the dates and points of interest for those interested in archaeology or timelines. This historical research has been done and can be accessed in other books. The goal of this book is to present the part of the human story contained in the scriptures and to present it in figures more than words when possible. The text is an effort to encourage the reader and provide some explanation where the diagrams are not easily understood.

This human story is of great interest because it is on going, our world now has more than seven billion inhabitants and each one has a stake in our common history. Knowing what prior generations experienced, including their struggles, helps us as we examine our own circumstances. We have some guidance as we seek to optimize our opportunities and work to contain or diminish our dilemmas. It is an old idea that encapsulates this, that those who do not examine the past are doomed to repeat it. This has not been proven as a historical axiom, but certainly one can learn a great deal from experiences, especially the joint human experience.

God has always had a special role in humanity's self-understanding. He is seen in creation. He was the standard for the human race that was created in His image. Human relationships can even mimic the relationships that people can have with the Creator. Human relationships are formed and are lasting based on the benefits and the motivations of the participants. In all this God has always ordered, arranged and allowed relationships. While we can see and feel love from God in this way we also notice that human relationships have a natural tendency to disorder, when this happens these relationships often disintegrate or fall apart. Studying the stories and relationships as they have been recorded in the Bible reminds us of why it is so crucial to understand this paradox of a loving God who allows human freedom. This book presents a structure to study the Bible and in an informed way to illuminate our own God-longings.

The focus of this book is to promote Bible reading and understanding, not to add to the already long list of religious books and materials. As a caution it should be stated that even the best publications, radio shows and other media can cloud rather than contribute to our knowledge of scriptural truths. This book presents information that is available in other forms drawn from other sources, including from readily available translations of the Bible, however the spelling that is presented here is from the NAS Bible. The material here traces human history by copying what is in the Bible and it is presented here as the lineage and purposeful plan God has always had for creation.

A reading of the Bible based on this structure of vertical connections to God as well as horizontal connections to people should lead to more productive and amenable relationships with fellow humans. Jesus summed it up as recorded in the book of Luke (it was named after the author of the account: Luke) in the tenth chapter,

Luke 10:25-28:

> And a lawyer stood up and put Him to the test, saying, "Teacher, what shall I do to inherit eternal life?"
> And He said to him, "What is written in the Law? How does it read to you?"
> And he answered, "YOU SHALL LOVE THE LORD YOUR GOD WITH ALL YOUR HEART, AND WITH ALL YOUR SOUL, AND WITH ALL YOUR STRENGTH, AND WITH ALL YOUR MIND; AND YOUR NEIGHBOR AS YOURSELF."
> And He said to him, "You have answered correctly; DO THIS AND YOU WILL LIVE."

As Luke records the observations of this interaction Jesus had with a lawyer, it instructs the reader's priorities. It was proper instruction for eager listeners then and Jesus' words have a ring that echoes in our ears today. Jesus simply states to read and learn from the scriptures. If the message is internalized, and what is learned is then applied to your life, there will be actions that come as a result. Jesus says, "Do this and you will live."

A Key

Mark	Meaning	Example
-	Denotes a marital relationship	Abram-Sarai (the two were husband and wife)
\, l, /	All three symbols denote a parental relationship	Adam-Eve, l Cain, Abel, Seth Adam and Eve were the parents of these three.
,	A comma denotes a sibling relationship when names are side by side	Cain, Abel, Seth

Chapter 1: The Beginning (Genesis)

```
                            Adam-Eve
                               |
                  Seth, Cain, Abel (killed by Cain)
                    |           |
                 Enosh        Enoch
                    |           |
                  Kenan        Irad
                    |           |
              Mahalalel     Mehujael
                  |           |
              Jared        Lamech (2 wives) -Adah -Zillah
                |                        |        |
         Enoch (never died)      Jabal, Jubal   Tubal-Cain, Naamah (daughter)
           |
         Methuselah (lived to be 969 years old)
           |
         Lamech
           |
         Noah (built and lived in the ark with his wife and 3 sons and their wives)
           |
         Shem, Ham (father of Canaan), Japheth
```

The Creator created a perfect world with specific instructions and a plan for humankind. This ended when sin entered the world, upon Adam and Eve's entanglement with the serpent. In the next generation murder occurs when Cain kills his brother out of jealousy and humankind descends into a meaningless downward spiral culminating in a world of oppression and evil. God stops this evil by sending a flood, in His mercy He selected Noah to save the world. Noah and his family along with animals survive the flood. God demonstrates His desire to save and restore through this story.

In the ninth chapter of the book of <u>Genesis</u>, God has some specific instructions and promises for Noah and his descendants, including the story of the rainbow found in verses 12 and 13 (I set My bow in the cloud). Genesis 9:2-7 states:

> "The fear of you and the terror of you will be on every beast of the earth and on every bird of the sky; with everything that creeps on the ground, and all the fish of the sea, into your hand they are given.
> "Every moving thing that is alive shall be food for you; I give all to you, as {I gave} the green plant.
> "Only you shall not eat flesh with its life, that is, its blood.
> "Surely I will require your lifeblood; from every beast I will require it. And from every man, from every man's brother I will require the life of man.
> "Whoever sheds man's blood, By man his blood shall be shed, For in the image of God He made man.
> "As for you, be fruitful and multiply; Populate the earth abundantly and multiply in it."

<u>The sons of Noah</u>

Shem was the first son of Noah:

```
                    Shem (the father of the children of Eber)
                             |
Elam, Asshur, Arpachshad (born 2 years after the flood), Lud, Aram
                    |                                            |
              Shelah                        Uz, Hul, Gether, Mash
                 |
            Eber
               |
        Peleg (The earth was divided in his time), Joktan*
             |
         Reu
            |
        Serug
           |
      Nahor
          |
    Terah
        |
Abram, -Sarai (different mother, Gen. 20:12), Nahor, Haran
```

*Joktan was the father of Almodad, Sheleph, Hazarmaveth, Jerah, Hadoram, Uzal, Diklah, Obal, Abimael, Sheba, Ophir, Havilah, Jobab.

The family tree of Terah is expanded in the following pages; Abram eventually is renamed Abraham and becomes the father of many nations. Sarai is the half sister of Abram and she becomes his wife, she is later renamed Sarah. In her old age Sarah gives birth to a son named Isaac, he was her only child.

Ham was the second son of Noah:

```
                    Ham
                     |
        Cush, Mizraim, Put, Canaan
```

These are the diverse descendants of Ham's sons Cush, Mizraim, Put and Canaan. The sons of Cush were Seba, Havilah, Sabta, Raamah, Sabteca, and Nimrod. There were peoples descended from each of these as outlined below,

-From the sons of Cush were Sheba, and Dedan.

-From the sons of Mizraim were Ludim, Anamim, Lehabim, Naphatahim, Puthrusim, Casluhim, and Caphtorim. There were the peoples descended from Mizraim, and this included the Philistines.

-The sons of Canaan were Sidon, and Heth. The peoples descended from Canaan were the Jebusites, Amorites, Girgashites, Hivites, Arkites, Sinites, Arvadites, Zemarites, and Hamathites.

Japheth was the third son of Noah:

```
                  Japheth
                     |
    Gomer, Magog, Madai, Javan, Tubal, Meshech, Tiras
         /                      \
Ashkenaz, Riphath, Togarmah    Elishah, Tarshish, Kittim, Dodanim
```

The earth was not populated as it is today at this point in human history. Genesis tells this story in chapter 11.

Reading from the Bible

Another key figure in the Bible thought to be of this same era was Job. His story is told in the Book of <u>Job</u>, it should be read at this point. Genesis should be read and Job should be read, alongside or right after Genesis.

<u>Abraham, the Patriarch</u>

Terah was the father of Abram:

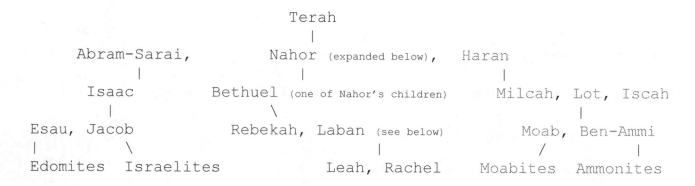

Isaac was a miracle child since Sarai had been barren before Isaac's birth. In Genesis (Gen.) Chapter 11, verses 31-32, Terah takes Abram and Lot then leaves from Ur, which was their home area. Terah reestablishes the family in Haran. The following events transpire,

In Gen. 12:1-4, Abram and Lot leave that area.

In Gen. 13:9, Abram and Lot separate.

In Gen. 11:27-17:4, the story of Abram is told.

In Gen. 17:5, Abram's name is changed to Abraham.

In Gen. 17:5-25:10, the story of Abraham is continued (his name was changed from Abram).

In Gen. 25:5-6, Abraham doles out his blessings.

Abraham's son of promise was Isaac who married his cousin Rebekah, she had twins who were not alike in any major way. The twins were named Jacob and Esau. They fought and rivaled each other from the womb. Jacob eventually married his cousins Leah and Rachel.

In the family tree above several people groups are mentioned, the Edomites are the descendants of Esau, and the Israelites are descended from Jacob. There are also the Ammonites and Moabites who are descended from Lot.

Abraham also had an older son, named Ishmael who became the father of the Ishmaelites. These peoples also figure in the later stories as the Bible story line is unraveled.

The family of Nahor:

```
Nahor-Milcah (daughter of Nahor's brother Haran)          -Reumah* (concubine)
       |
Uz, Buz, Kemuel, Chesed, Hazo, Pildash, Jidlah, Bethuel
        |                                           |
     Aram                              Rebekah (married Isaac), Laban
                                                                  |
                                                           Leah, Rachel
```

Nahor married his niece, Milcah and a concubine named Reumah. Milcah was the daughter of Haran. Haran was her husband's brother. She became the grandmother of Rebekah, who became Isaac's wife. Milcah's descendants married back into Abraham's line since Rebekah married Isaac and then also Jacob's wives, named Leah and Rachel came from this family. More specifically, Milcah's grandson Laban has two girls named Leah and Rachel who marry Jacob. Laban thus becomes Jacob's father-in-law.

*The Descendants of Nahor and his concubine Reumah are Tebah, Gaham, Tahash, and Maacah.

The family of Haran:

```
                              Haran
                                |
                   Milcah (marries Nahor), Lot, Iscah
                  /                          |
(see Nahor's family)              Moab, Ben-Ammi
```

Lot is the nephew of Abraham and leaves with him to travel to the land God promised to Abraham.

Lot eventually loses everything except his two daughters when the punishment falls on Sodom.

Lot's family:

```
        Lot-wife (she turned into a pillar of salt upon fleeing Sodom)
            |
1st daughter , 2nd daughter (follows her sister)
|                            |
Moab                      Ben-Ammi
|                            |
Moabites                  Ammonites
```

Lot was Abraham's nephew, his father, Haran and Abraham were brothers. Lot escaped the destruction of Sodom, he lost his wife on the way and went to live in the hills. He became drunk and fathered two children, Moab and Ben-Ammi. Moab was born to Lot's first daughter. Ben-Ammi was born to Lot's second daughter. Moab became the father of the Moabites and Ben-Ammi became the father of the Ammonites. Lot's descendants eventually become rivals of the Israelite descendants of Abraham. Later in the biblical generations, one of Lot's descendants marries into the line of King David; her name was Ruth, she was a Moabitess. Her story is in the book of Ruth.

Bethuel's family:

```
                    Bethuel (son of Nahor and Milcah; he is Abraham's nephew)
                                |
               Rebekah (married Isaac), Laban
              /                          \
  Esau,   Jacob (marries Leah and Rachel)    Leah, Rachel, other sons
  |         |
Edomites  Israelites
```

The Family

Abraham's family is the story of the remainder of the Bible. Abraham has many children but his heir is Isaac. Isaac was born to Abraham by his wife Sarah after many years of childlessness. Isaac took a wife from his mother and father's home area she was named Rebekah. Rebekah was the daughter of his cousin Bethuel. Rebekah had twins, they were named Jacob and Esau. Jacob became the heir of Isaac and Rebekah; he carries on the family name as the grandson of Abraham.

Jacob had to leave the area he grew up in, he flees because he has stolen Esau's rights as first born. He left on bad terms with his brother Esau. Jacob conspired a ruse and he left after plotting to fool his father and then stealing his brother's rights. Although they were twins Esau had been born first. Jacob accomplished this theft by disguising himself in stolen clothing and animal skin, tricking his father Isaac.

When Jacob left he went to the area his mother came from, that is to the land of Terah's descendants. In this land he came to his mother's family to look for a wife. He goes to his uncle Laban to find a wife and he lives with Laban for several years. Jacob worked for Laban and was a successful pastoralist. Jacob married Leah first then Rachel second and they had a large family. Jacob's family became a clan. It grew as Jacob had children with four women and these children each had families of their own. As the families grow, Jacob becomes the father of the twelve tribes of Israel. They were called Israelites.

Esau married several women including the daughter of his uncle Ishmael who was the older brother of his father Isaac. Esau became the father of the Edomites.

Abraham's expanded family tree:

```
Abram (Abraham)-Hagar (Sarah's servant) -Sarai (renamed Sarah) -Keturah
   |                                        |                      |
Ishmael,                                  Isaac,      many children (below)
   |                                        |
12 princes (below)                   Esau, Jacob (renamed Israel)
```

The sons of Ishmael were Nebaioth, Kedar, Adbeel, Mibsam, Mishma, Dumah, Massa, Hadad, Tema, Jetur, Naphish, and Kedemah. Ishmael also had a daughter named Basemath who later married Esau.

Jacob and Esau were twins but Esau was born first. Esau should have gained and inherited from his father, but Jacob tricked their father Isaac. He supplanted his brother and Isaac was duped into giving Jacob the blessings of a first-born. This caused a great deal of friction between the brothers. Jacob and Esau later reconciled when Jacob returned from living with Laban (his maternal uncle and father-in-law). The descendants of Jacob, who are called the Israelites later become rivals with the descendants of Esau, the Edomites.

The story of the family of Esau can be found in several passages including, Genesis 26:34. More information on Esau's family is in 1 Chronicles 1, Genesis 28:8-9, and Genesis 36. The descendants of Esau moved to the region of Mt Seir. Esau married into Ishmael's family to try to please his parents but he also married Oholibamah the daughter of Anah and the granddaughter of Zibeon the Hivite. Esau had several wives altogether. These were his sons born in that land of Canaan, Eliphaz, Reuel (grandson of Ishmael), Jeush, Jalam and Korah.

Ishmael had a large family. Isaac only had two sons but they each went on to have large families. Abraham also took another wife after Sarah died, her name was Keturah and had many children with her. Abraham's direct descendants were very numerous.

Abraham and Keturah:

```
                    Abraham-Keturah
                          |
      Zimran, Jokshan, Medan, Midian, Ishbak, Shuah
               |                    |
         Sheba, Dedan          Ephah, Epher, Hanoch, Abida, Eldaah
               |
Asshurim, Letushim, Leummim
```

The House of Israel

In Genesis Chapter 35, verse 10, God renames Jacob. It is recorded, "but Israel shall be your name." Israel (Jacob) has 12 sons, who form the 12 tribes of Israel.

These are mothers of Jacob's children and the birth orders of their children:

```
-Leah (1st wife) -Zilpah (2nd concubine) -Rachel (2nd wife) -Bilhah (1st concubine)
|                 |                        |                  |
1 Reuben          7 Gad       11 Joseph                     5 Dan
2 Simeon          8 Asher     12 Benoni (called Benjamin)   6 Naphtali
3 Levi
4 Judah
9 Issachar
10 Zebulun
Dinah (a daughter, she was older than Joseph and Benjamin)
```

See Genesis 34 for the story of Dinah.

See Genesis 38 for the story of Judah and his sons, including Perez.

Joseph

Joseph, the first born son of Rachel and Jacob, was sold down to Egypt by his brothers. Eventually, the whole family moved there to a region called Goshen during a great famine. The Israelites lived in Egypt for several generations and did not leave Egypt until the time of Moses.

See Genesis 37, 39-50 for the story of Joseph, who was sold into slavery in Egypt. Joseph was falsely accused by his master's wife and was thrown into prison. He was very capable in all that he did and even in prison he performed all the work he was given.

Joseph was a dreamer and an interpreter of dreams. In Genesis 41:15-37, he helped Pharaoh by giving him God's answer to his dream. He was released from prison after helping the Pharaoh and tasked with preparing for the predicted seven years of famine. He thrived in Egypt and governed a great public health success.

Joseph's brothers came to him for help during the time of great famine. Unbeknownst to them, the brother they had sold into slavery, had become second in charge of all Egypt. Upon reconciling, Joseph's brothers and all their families and father eventually relocated to Egypt because of the great famine. This great famine was mitigated by Joseph's preparation. Seventy male members of the family of Jacob came to Egypt. Joseph created a haven for his family in a region of Egypt called Goshen. Joseph marries Asenath and has two sons, Manasseh and Ephraim. These two sons become the founders of half tribes in the Israelite family. See Gen. 49 for Jacob's (Israel's) blessing of his descendants.

Chapter 2: The Exodus

In Exodus 1:8, a new ruler came to power in Egypt that had never heard of Joseph. This new Pharaoh feared the Israelites and implemented harsh constraints on them. By this point the Israelites had become very numerous. In Exodus chapter 2, the story of Moses begins; he is one of the great-grandsons of Levi born in Egypt. By now the sons of Israel have become so numerous that Pharaoh puts inhumane and evil population control measures in place. Moses was placed in a basket and hidden in the river when he was a baby to avoid these murderous measures. Moses had a brother Aaron and he had a sister named Miriam.

Moses became a son of Egypt when he was found in his basket floating on the Nile River by the daughter of the Pharaoh. He was raised in the ruler's house. When he grew up and became old enough he tried to take matters into his own hands and he killed an Egyptian overlord who was mistreating one of the Israelite slaves. When the matter became known, Moses fled Egypt and went to live in the desert. He rescued some women who are watering their sheep from the competing livestock tenders. The women were the daughters of Jethro. Moses later married Zipporah, a daughter of Jethro.

Moses' story includes:

-Adoption by Pharaoh's daughter,

-Killing of an Egyptian and subsequent flight,

-An encounter with a burning bush,

-Plagues in Egypt,

-Parting of the Red Sea,

-10 commandments, and the law,

-Counts of the people at different points (including all the warriors in Numbers 1),

-The blessing, and songs of Moses.

Exodus through Deuteronomy recounts the period of about 40 years when the Israelites left Egypt and went to the Promised Land. This was the land that had been shown and promised to Abraham, Isaac and Jacob as an inheritance for their descendants. Moses and his brother Aaron were the leaders of the Israelites. In the next generation the Israelites followed Joshua, who was Moses' servant.

The book of Leviticus carefully records all the laws that God gave Moses for the people. The book of Numbers recounts the journey and wandering through the wilderness regions. During this time the people were prepared for the military overthrow of the inhabitants of the Promised Land.

The book of Deuteronomy records a return to the theme of the law of God. It records God's instructions through Moses, it is the second giving of the law. Moses passed on all the instructions of the Lord to the Israelites. These instructions were applied to all areas of life and guided the people from that time through the time of the judges. The law of God was used on through the time of the kings, and into the exile. Of course these laws and their interpretation continue to be used. The law is used by devotees of these careful instructions for guidance and direction even today.

Reading from the Bible

Up to this point in the Biblical story one should have read Genesis, Job, Exodus, Leviticus, Numbers, *and* Deuteronomy. *This lays the foundation for the rest of the Bible.*

A Short Outline

A short outline could be constructed of the Bible to this point. It would include a list from Adam, Noah, Abraham to Moses. Adam's story shows the love of God and the design intended for nature. The story also includes the record of the first sin (disobedience) and the consequences of sin. Noah's story shows that God has a plan to deliver His people. The story of Abraham shows how a fully devoted follower of God operates by faith and obedience even in difficult circumstances. Genesis contains the account from the beginning and the personal stories of Adam, through Noah, to Abraham, Isaac and Jacob.

Moses' life shows the power of God when He chooses to use a leader for His purposes. Moses was preserved, educated and trained despite being born into a slave family. In Deuteronomy chapter 34, the story of the last account of Moses on earth is recorded. He was buried by his countrymen at a ripe old age. He started his ministry at the age of 80 and served the Lord until his death.

Job contains the story of one man's efforts to follow the Lord whole heartedly even in hardship. The story proves that God is not a god to be manipulated. Job's story shows that while God blesses those who trust and follow Him, His ways are higher and those who do not experience blessing on Earth are not necessarily evil. Every difficulty is not a sign of God's punishment for evil acts. People who experience these difficult things or find themselves in the midst of tragedy are not necessarily being punished for their sins. Sin leads to destruction and death, but not every difficulty is because of a person's sin, it may be due to wider sin in the world or in the case of Job, an evil accuser. God is a God of perfect justice, but from the human perspective without all the information, this is hard to see especially in the midst of hardship. Job experiences some of the worst hardships imaginable, his story shows that those who are experiencing hardship or even death cannot be said to be enemies of God simply by looking at their circumstances. God is just in every instance but His timing and the reasons why He moves as He does are sometimes a mystery to us. Job is a wonderful example of persevering in faith.

The Sacrifices

Moses was given all the instructions for right living and worship. The list of ritual sacrifices was in several broad categories. There were peace, burnt, sin and guilt offerings offered at the Tabernacle. Each had it's own specific format. A general pattern was that an animal or a grain offering was brought to the priests in attendance at the altar. The priests followed specific handling regulations for the animals. The priests would offer parts or the whole animal as a sacrifice. The priests prepared and burnt parts or the whole offering on the altar depending on the type of sacrifice or offering being offered.

A sacrifice involved several steps, it started with a clean animal (a ruminant with split hooves) that was brought to the Tabernacle. The Tabernacle was a tent carefully put together according to the instructions Moses had received from God. The sacrifices were later brought to the Temple built by King Solomon in Jerusalem.

The person making the sacrifice or bringing an offering brought the offering and laid a hand on it's head. This signified that the animal was replacing the individual. Then the animal was killed, skinned, and chopped up. It's blood was then sprinkled, this meant blood over the altar, and in some cases the blood was also placed as a symbol on other items or persons. The animal was then burned on the altar.

Initially this location of sacrifice was in the Tabernacle tent. This tent was created by the Israelites at God's instruction. It was taken down and moved with them through the wilderness and on into the Promised Land, at each stop it was reassembled. When the time came to break camp and move along the route the tent would be taken down according to specific instructions by appointed families. The Tabernacle and the parts were carried on to the next site by the tribe of Levi. This was a big task but it was divided into segments with assignments for different families, making it easier accomplish the various movements. It was eventually moved to Jerusalem and under King David was the nation's site of sacrifices. King Solomon then built a permanent place for the sacrifices by constructing a Temple. The Temple was destroyed and rebuilt under various oppressors until the Roman destruction of the site in 70AD.

A Table comparing the sacrifices and offerings.

Sacrifice	Process	Blood	Occasion
Burnt	Animal was brought to the Tabernacle, a hand laid on it's head, it was killed, skinned, chopped up, and the blood sprinkled over the altar. The animal was burned on the altar.	Poured out at the foot of the altar.	Most common, official act of worship in Tabernacle and later Temple. As acts of private devotion by individuals often with sin or guilt offering.
Peace	Animal was brought to the Tabernacle, a hand laid on it's head, killed, skinned, chopped up, sprinkled blood over the altar, burned animal on the altar. Some was eaten by the Priests and worshippers.	Poured out at the foot of the altar.	Prescribed with the feast of weeks (Pentecost), also given at dedications, since the meat was shared with all, it became a very festive event. Also called freewill offerings, to be offered at any time. This type of offering was also prescribed to prevent the sacrifice of animals to other spirits in the fields and alternative places (Leviticus 17).
Guilt (also reparation)	Animal was brought to the Tabernacle, a hand laid on it's head, killed, skinned, chopped up, sprinkled blood over the altar, burned the animal on the altar. Some of the meat could be eaten by the Priests.	Poured out at the foot of the altar.	Not part of the normal routine of official sacrifices. Offered for serious sins such as sacrilege, the breach of a Nazirite vow (Lev 5:14-6:7, 19:20-22, Numbers 6:9-12). Former lepers had to offer this offering.

Sacrifice	Process	Blood	Occasion
Sin (also purification)	Animal was brought to the Tabernacle, a hand laid on it's head, killed, skinned, chopped up, sprinkled blood over the altar, burned the animal on the altar. Some of the meat could be eaten by the Priests.	Smeared on the altar or other parts of the Tabernacle	Regular, but less common part of regular worship, also offered by individuals after uncleanness.
Other items	Grains, cereals, meal, oil, wine. Handful or more could be burnt, the rest given to the Priests.	The wine was poured out at the foot of the altar like blood.	Often with other sacrifices or if one was too poor to afford an animal.

Chapter 3: The Succession

Joshua who was Moses' servant became the leader of the Israelites when he inherited leadership from Moses as recorded in Joshua chapter 1. Joshua was a military leader who later became the head of the people after Moses' death. At this point in the Israelite journey from Egypt to the Promised Land, Joshua's family, and Caleb's family are the only survivors of their generation left. This was because Joshua and Caleb were the only two spies, sent out to scout the Promised Land, who believed that it could be obtained with God's help. There were spies selected out of each tribe, so Joshua and Caleb were the only two out of the twelve, who were originally selected. Everyone else of that generation died during the years of wandering in the wilderness, because they did not agree with Joshua and Caleb and trust that they could win a great victory. Their children lived on and inherited the Promised Land under Joshua's leadership, this episode of espionage is recorded in the book of Numbers chapter 13 and following.

Moses was a spiritual father to Joshua his servant, Joshua's physical father was named Nun; Caleb was Joshua's spiritual brother. Joshua was from the tribe of Ephraim. Joshua led a generation of new Israelites in the conquest of the Promised Land starting with Jericho. Rahab and her family were the only survivors of Jericho. Joshua's last words are recorded in Joshua 24. The book of Joshua shows us that God provides a savior for His people.

Reading from the Bible

Up to this point in the Biblical story one should have read Genesis, Job, Exodus, Leviticus, Numbers, Deuteronomy and Joshua.

The Judges

After Joshua there was an era when Israel was guided by judges, see Judges 2:16. The first three chapters of Judges show the transition from Joshua to the judges. Some of the judges in this inheritance, who delivered the Israelites and had authority over them are included in this list, Othniel (He was Caleb's nephew, and became his son-in-law), Ehud, Shamgar, Deborah (a prophetess, who combined with Barak in a great battle of deliverance). There was then,

Gideon
|
Abimelech (Gideon's son, he seizes power after Gideon, Israel first flirts with the idea of an earthy ruler or king in Gideon's time, see Judges 8:22). Others that judged include,

Tola, Jair, Jephthah (he reviews part of the exodus history while in discourse with an enemy king), Ibzan, Elon, Abdon, and Samson.

The status of Israel after the death of Samson is found in Judges 17:6, it tells us that the condition of Israel is difficult and a condition of disarray. There were twelve tribes and their territories were far flung and the unity between them was at times tenuous. The spiritual hub was Shiloh where the Tabernacle was pitched, but many of the Israelites are not devoted followers of God and do not visit this site for ritual sacrifices and worship.

Table of the Judges

Judge	Enemies	Comment	Rule
Othniel	Mesopotamians	He was the nephew and son in-law of Caleb, Chapters 1-3	40 years
Ehud	Eglon, King of Moab	He was a Benjamite, Chapter 3	The land was undisturbed for 80 years
Shamgar	Philistines	Chapter 3	
Deborah/Barak	Jabin, the King of Canaan, and Sisera the commander of Jabin's army	Deborah was the wife of Lappidoth, Chapters 4-5	The land was undisturbed for 40 years
Gideon	Midianites, and Amalekites, from the East	Chapters 6-8	
Abimelech	Infighting and evil	Chapter 9	3 years
Tola		He was the son of Puah, a man of Issachar, Chapter 10	23 years
Jair		He was a Gileadite (east of the Jordan River), Chapter 10	22 years
Jephthah	Ammonites	Gileadite (east of the Jordan), Chapters 11-12	6 years
Ibzan		He was from Bethlehem, Chapter 12	7 years
Elon		Zebulunite, Chapter 12	10 years
Abdon		Chapter 12	8 years
Samson	Philistines	Danite, son of Manoah, Chapters 13-16	20 years

During the time of the Judges, Ruth the Moabitess becomes a descendant of Abraham, see Ruth 1:16-17. Ruth was a widow, who had been married to a man from the territory of Judah. Her husband's name was Mahlon; he died in Moab. Ruth's husband was the son of Elimelech and Naomi. They were an Israelite couple who had migrated to the land of Moab during a time of famine. Ruth later left her homeland with her widowed Mother-in-law when Naomi wished to return to her home territory. Ruth found favor and was married to Boaz, her kinsman redeemer (see Leviticus 25, verse 23 and following, also Deuteronomy 25, verses 5 through 9). The book of Judges reminds us of God's law and the standards He holds for all peoples. God shows Himself to be a God of justice, mercy and restoration.

Ruth left her family in Moab to return with Naomi to Bethlehem after the death of her husband, brother-in-law and Father-in-law. She demonstrated an understanding of the Mosaic law and culture by participating in the harvest ritual of the impoverished which included gleaning as recorded in Leviticus 19. She was noted as a woman of honor and she followed the instruction of her Mother-in-law to become a fully devoted follower of God. The book of Ruth shows us that God's love is limitless and He provides for His people. He brings people into His family, using them in extraordinary ways.

Reading from the Bible

To this point in the reading of the Bible, one should have read through the books of Judges and Ruth.

The line of Boaz (a descendant of Judah):

```
Abraham
  |
Isaac
  |
Jacob
  |
Judah
  |
Perez
  |
Hezron
  |
Ram
  |
Amminadab
  |
Nahshon                                  The Prophet Samuel's lineage:
  |
Salmon-Rahab (a woman from Jericho)      Elkanah-Hannah (second of two wives)
  |                                           |
Boaz-Ruth                                Samuel (dedicated to the Lord early by his mother)
  |                                           |
Obed (who brought joy to Naomi)          Joel, Abijah
  |
Jesse
  |
David (killed Goliath and later became King of Israel)
```

At the end of the time of the judges there was a priest named Eli and he had an apprentice named Samuel. Samuel became a great leader for the Israelites. The Prophet Samuel was a contemporary of King Saul and King David. Samuel's mother prayed for a child earnestly and was blessed by Samuel's birth. She dedicated him to the Lord and he served the Lord his whole life. Samuel like Boaz and Ruth came out of a difficult time in the history of the Israelites, a period of great apostasy. The people often were evil in the Israelite territory and as the people did evil they came under oppressors. It was in this time that God would send judges who ruled over regions of the Promised Land.

Samuel served the Lord whole heartedly but his sons did not and the people saw that the sons of Samuel were unfit judges. These sons were corrupt and perverted, this caused the people in the nation of Israel to cry out for a king. Samuel, with God's direction chose and anointed Saul as recorded in 1 Samuel (Sam) chapter 10 verse 1. This anointing signaled that Saul was God's chosen one. Saul established himself as recorded in 1 Samuel 11.

King Saul eventually became disobedient and lost favor with God, in particular for not following the sacrificial requirements. David the son of Jesse, increased in favor with God and in popularity with the people, he was anointed as the new king in 1 Samuel 16. David tried to serve King Saul and even became fast friends with Jonathan who was Saul's son. Saul came to perceive David as a rival and drove him away so that he had to live in hiding and exile. After Saul's death his son Ish-bosheth briefly became king, although the tribe of Judah rejected Saul's son and instead followed David. Samuel was the last of his era, after him the nation was led by kings. The kings ruled over Israel, first King Saul, then under King David's line and finally in a divided kingdom.

Reading from the Bible

The reading to this point is in 1 Samuel, and 2 Samuel.

Chapter 4: The Kings

King Saul was from the tribe of Benjamin:

```
                              Aphiah
                                |
                             Becorath
                                |
                              Zeror
                                |
                              Abiel
                                |
                         Kish, Ner  (father of Abner)
                                |
                     Saul  (became King after the anointing by Samuel)
                                |
        Jonathan, Abinadab, Malchishua, Ish-bosheth, Merab, Michal
            |
Merib-baal, Mephibosheth
 |
Micah
 |
Pithon, Melech, Tarea, Ahaz
                            |
                         Jehoaddah
                            |
            Alemeth, Azmaveth, Zimri
                            |
                          Moza
                            |
                          Binea
                            |
                         Raphah
                            |
                        Eleasah
                            |
                         Azel
                            |
Azrikam, Bocheru, Ishmael, Sheariah, Obadiah, Hanan
```

Saul was married to Ahinoam the daughter of Ahimaaz. Saul was also the father of Ishvi and

Eshbaal; his daughters were Merab and Michal. Saul's cousin Abner served as his general of the

army. Saul's sons, Jonathan, Abinadab, and Malchishua died with their father Saul, while fighting against the Philistines. Ish-bosheth, the son of Saul was made king for two years after Saul's death, by Abner. Abner was the son of Ner and the grandson of Abiel. Ner and Kish were brothers.

Saul had two sons with a concubine named Rizpah. These two sons were named Armoni and Mephibosheth. They were handed over along with Saul's five grandsons (born to Saul's daughter Merab and her husband Barzillai) to be hanged by the people that King Saul had oppressed wrongfully. King David handed them over as an act of retribution. King David buried Saul and Jonathan as well as the seven who were hanged, in the grave of Saul's father, Kish. King David spared Jonathan's son Mephibosheth from hanging and showed kindness to Mephibosheth because of his great love for Jonathan and a vow he had made to him.

King David's son, named Solomon, ruled over the whole of Israel after him. All the tribes were unified under one king and the wealth of Israel was pronounced. They were also able to build a cohesive nation around the Temple built in Jerusalem. The line of Saul never came into leadership again.

David's line continued to rule after him. The nation of Israel was united under Saul, then David and Solomon. The Israelite Kingdom split at the end of King Solomon's reign. The kings in David's line ruled over the Tribe of Judah in the south of the Promised Land. The 10 tribes with territories in the North and East split off and formed the nation of Israel. The Southern Kingdom was call the Kingdom of Judah. Judah included Jerusalem and so there were members of all the tribes coming there; they were drawn to the Temple as pilgrims. In the Northern Kingdom different men came to power as kings over the Northern Kingdom. There was some intermarriage of the two royal lines in Israel and Judah. They had some political cooperations and varying degrees of cooperation in trade but there were also wars and animosity. The Northern Kingdom was eventually conquered and carried away into exile by the Assyrians. The Southern Kingdom was also later conquered by the Babylonians and the people of both kingdoms were eventually carried away into exile. This happened at different times, it came first for the Northern Kingdom and then after several generations the Southern Kingdom was also exiled.

Reading from the Bible

For the reader, portions of scripture from the part of the Old Testament called 'the writings and the prophets' can be added into the sections to enrich the reading. The first book of the collection of <u>Psalms</u> *(this includes Psalm 1 through 41) can be included here. A suggested reading list:*

1 Kings chapters 1-10, Psalms 1-41 (Book 1)

1 Kings chapters 11-22, Psalms 42-72 (Book 2)

Proverbs, Ecclesiastes, Song of Solomon

2 Kings, Jonah,

1 Chronicles, Psalms 73-150 (Book 3, 4, 5).

King David was from the tribe of Judah:

```
Boaz-Ruth
 |
Obed
 |
Jesse (Jesse had eight sons, he was an Ephrathite, from Bethlehem in Judah)
 |
Eliab, Abinadab, Shammah, David (became the second king of Israel)
```

Eliab, Abinadab, and Shammah were Jesse's three eldest sons. All of Jesse's sons in order were: Eliab, Abinadab, Shammah (Shimei), Nethanel, Raddai, Ozem and David. Jesse also had two daughters: Zeruiah and Abigail. Zeruiah was the mother of Abshai, Joab and Asahel.

David had several wives including Ahinoam the Jezreelitess, Abigail the widow of Nabal the Carmelite, and Bathsheba (the wife of Uriah). He became the father of many children including Amnon, Tamar, Absalom (who briefly over threw his father), Jedidiah (Solomon) and Adonijah. Adonijah was the son of Haggith, he was born after Absalom, and with the help of Joab he briefly proclaimed himself king at the end of David's reign. He was unsuccessful as God's promise was that Solomon should reign as king. Solomon was the second child of David and Bathsheba. He was identified as the rightful heir and the kingdom was turned over to him. He ruled as king after his father David in Jerusalem, he fortified the nation by building on what his father had done. David loved God wholeheartedly and was richly blessed.

Reading from the Bible

The reading list continued:

2 Chronicles chapters 1-26, Isaiah chapters 1-6, Micah,

2 Chronicles chapters 27-31, Nahum, Hosea, Isaiah chapters 7-44,

2 Chronicles chapters 32-33, Amos, Isaiah chapters 45-52, Obadiah, Zephaniah,

2 Chronicles chapters 34-36.

Kings & Prophets:

The Kings of Israel are depicted to the right below and those of Judah to the left. The Prophets of note are listed with the kings or rulers they advised.

Unified Kingdom

```
                        Saul              Prophets: Samuel
                         |
                     Ish-bosheth
```

David-Bathsheba   **Nathan**
|

Solomon-Naamah (Ammonitess)   Nebat (father of Jeroboam, he was never king)
| | Northern Kingdom (Israel)

Rehoboam (the kingdom splits)   **Ahijah**   Jeroboam (raised up to seize Israel, sinful)
| Southern Kingdom (Judah) |

Abijam (sinful, warred with Jeroboam) **Jehu**   Nadab (did evil)
|

Asa (did right, warred with Baasha)   Baasha (kills Nadab, seizes control, did evil)
| |

Jehosphat (did right)   Elah (sinful, reigned two years)
| **Micaiah**   Zimri (killed Elah, committed suicide)

Jehoram (did evil married Ahab's daughter)   Tibni vied with Omri(prevailed, evil)
| **Jahaziel** |

Ahaziah (did evil)   **Elijah**   Ahab (did evil)-Jezebel
David's line interrupted   **Elisha** |

Athaliah (mother of Ahaziah, seized control)   Ahaziah (did evil), Joram (did evil)

Johoash (son of Ahaziah, did right)   Jehu (killed Joram and Ahaziah, no heed to law)
| |

Amaziah (fought Joash, did right)   Jehoahaz (did evil)
| |

Azariah (Uzziah, did what was right)   Joash (did evil)
| |

               Jeroboam II (did evil)
Jonah (son of Ammittai) |

             Zechariah (did evil)

          Shallum (killed Zechariah ruled in his place)

Jotham (son of Uzziah, did what was right)   Menahem (killed Shallum, did evil)
| |

Ahaz (did not do what was right)   Pekahiah (did evil)
| Pekah (did evil, tribe of Naphtali captured)

Hezekiah (did what was right)   Hoshea (did evil, all Israel was carried away)
| **Isaiah** (son of Amoz)   Exile of Israel

Manasseh (mother was Hephzibah, he did evil, then repented)
|

Amon (did evil)-Jedidah (daughter of Adaiah of Bozkath)
|

Josiah (did right)   **Huldah** (a prophetess)
| **Jeremiah**

Joahaz, Jehoiakim (Eliakim, Pharaoh Neco changed his name, 2 Chronicles 36)
|

Jehoiachin (did evil)

Zedekiah (uncle of Jehoiachin, made king by Nebuchadnezzar, did evil, eventually overthrown and a governor was appointed in his place)
Exile of Judah

Gedailiah was the son of Ahikam, and grandson of Shaphan. He became governor of the remnant left behind after the people of Judah were taken away into exile.

The kingdom split during the reign of Solomon's son Rehoboam. Jeroboam, the son of Nebat became the first king of the Northern Kingdom of Israel. The kingdom split along mostly tribal lines. The Southern Kingdom called Judah was formed from the southern territory including Jerusalem and the territory of the tribes of Simeon, Judah, and Benjamin. There were also members of other tribes who moved to the Southern Kingdom because of their adherence to the temple sacrifices and ritual beliefs. The Northern Kingdom included the territory of the tribes of Asher, Naphtali, Zebulun, Gad, Dan, Manasseh, Ephraim, Reuben, and Issachar. The tribe of Levi had small territories, consisting only of cities of refuge and otherwise had smaller land holdings as part of their priestly duties, they were spread throughout the territory of the North and South.

Jeroboam's line did not retain the throne in the Northern Kingdom since they did not follow the instructions they were given. Various other men were raised up at various times to rule the kingdom of Israel until the reign of King Hoshea. The reign of King Hoshea ended because the country was overrun and all the people of the Northern Kingdom of Israel were carried away into exile.

The Northern Kingdom had a very tumultuous succession of kings. Omri was able to have multiple descendants on the throne in the Northern Kingdom. Jehu also had a small lineage that followed him as king, otherwise the succession was often a result of revolt or an overthrow of the king. Many of the Northern kings had very short reigns. The kings were often not concerned with justice and doing right. In many cases they were unjust rulers and frequently led the people poorly. One way this damaged the people was in the making of bad alliances. The evil and lack of justice eventually led to the downfall of the nation. The kingdom of Israel was overpowered and carried

away to exile during Hoshea's time; he was the last king of Israel. The kingdom of Judah

continued on and was in place until the time of the Babylonian conquest several generations later.

There were numerous prophets who prophesied during the time of kings including, Samuel,

Nathan, Ahijah, Jehu, Micaiah, Jahaziel, Elijah, Elisha, Jonah, Isaiah, Huldah, and Jeremiah. Some

of these prophets were also authors of books that were preserved. They are sometimes called the

'major' prophets. Others left shorter writings and are the 'minor' prophets. They served as

counselors and moral authorities for the kings with varying degrees of cooperation from the secular

powers.

The end of the kingdoms came at different times; first the Northern Kingdom (Israel) was

captured by the Assyrians. Then the Assyrians yielded to the Babylonians and their king, the great

Nebuchadnezzar. The Southern Kingdom (Judah) was in dire straits towards the end and they tried

to make alliances with Egypt to alleviate their desperate situation. These political realities are

discussed in the books written by Prophet <u>Jeremiah</u>.

After King Josiah's reign, there were two of his sons who ruled: Joahaz (deposed by Neco

the king of Egypt) and Jehoiakim whose name was changed from Eliakim. Jehoiakim became

king, but did evil and was captured by Nebuchadnezzar. The Promised Land became a vassal or

province of the great Babylonian empire which extended to the Brook of Egypt in the West. All the

land and wealth built up during the time of David and Solomon had become the property of others

and all that was left was a remnant of the poor and weak.

Among the kings of Judah, Josiah stands out as someone who lived up to the reputation of

his ancestor David. David is the standard by which the kings are measured since he followed God whole heartedly and even in his failings repented and sought forgiveness. Josiah was able to lead his generation in repentance and to implement right religious patterns. King Ahab of the Northern Kingdom stands in contrast as one who did evil and even arranged for someone's murder upon his wife's advice to gain additional land. He is a foil to Elijah the prophet and seeks to kill him on several occasions.

Reading from the Bible

The reading up to this point includes the Prophets. A suggested guide includes the following books, Isaiah chapters 53-66, Jeremiah, Lamentations, Habakkuk.

Chapter 5: Time of exile, the Writings and the Prophets

Ezra and Nehemiah both led back expeditions from exile to rebuild Jerusalem and the Temple. Their story is in the two books bearing their names. These two books go together and tell the story of the rebuilding of Jerusalem. Zerubbabel was the first to lead a group back to the Promised Land. Ezra also returns from exile and served as the spiritual leader. Nehemiah returned still later and was the governor. Ezra was a direct descendant of Aaron, Moses' brother. These two books show God's care and love towards His people as He restores them. God shows Himself to be ready for restoration and this affects both the spiritual and physical states of His followers.

Esther is the story of Jewish life in exile. Her story is a story of faithfulness and the stewardship of God's blessings and provision. She stands up to a threat on the lives of the Jews and is used to safeguard the people in exile.

Job's placement chronologically, is not known, the setting fits with the times of Abraham.

Psalms is a collection of Poems and songs written by several writers including King David and King Solomon. These poems and songs cover many of life's problems and pitfalls. There are numerous themes woven throughout the collection, it could be said that the Psalms contain some of the most real, intimate themes of the whole Bible. The collection can also be divided into five books. The teaching in each Psalm can stand alone to be learned from although there are themes and common threads through the Psalter. Psalms 1 and 2 introduce the Psalter and lay out the theme of destruction for the wicked and reward for the people who practice right living. The collection stands as a loud call to God-seekers, it is an admonition to return to the theme of love for the Creator and of God's ongoing dealings in the world. The authors describe their hopes in the Lord, their realities and their difficulties. The collection is as real as it gets with numerous scenarios described that mirror real life situations met in all historical ages. The Psalms show the reader how to praise God for who He is and what He has done in all circumstances, with every breath.

Proverbs, Ecclesiastes and Song of Solomon form a collection of wisdom and poetry from King Solomon. These writings serve as a collection to guide the reader in life's seasons and show that God's hand is never far for those who seek His guidance and assurance. Ecclesiastes chapter 3 verse 11 tells us that God creates humans with a sense of eternity. Even with this sense however we are not able to comprehend all that God is or all that He accomplishes.

Isaiah was a prophet during the latter half of the time of kings. His work is rich and gives a window into heaven. He also describes God's plan to send a suffering servant to save His people. Isaiah chapter 56 reminds the reader that God has a broad and diverse people to call His own.

Jeremiah was a prophet during the end of the kingdom of Judah. Lamentations was also written by Jeremiah. These books detail the evil and wrong perpetrated by the Israelites before the final destruction of their kingdom. It serves as a reminder of the futility and inevitable end of sin, a reminder to turn from it and come into a pattern of right living.

Ezekiel contains the story of the time of exile, it was written during the time of exile. Ezekiel paints a picture that reminds the reader of God's dealings with His people and a plan to bring them back to a right relationship with Him. God explains in Ezekiel chapter 36 that He will bring His Spirit to guide the steps of His followers.

Daniel contains the story of the young man named Daniel who was part of the conquest of Judah by Nebuchadnezzar. He was taken as a captive, he lived in exile and he was there when the Babylonians yielded to the Medes and Persians. Daniel leaves a great personal example for integrity and right conduct even in difficult circumstances. Daniel also saw visions and foretold the future. These writings remind the reader that upright living and doing what is right can put them at odds with the prevailing culture and even lead to suffering at the hands of unjust leaders. The book of Daniel records the story of a life of longevity and faithfulness in the service of the Heavenly King while being faithful and dedicated to working hard for the earthly authorities.

Hosea was a prophet during the time of kings. Hosea, Amos, Jonah and Micah are thought by scholars to belong to the Neo-Assyrian period (Hill & Walton, p. 462). The story of Hosea reminds the reader of the danger and repugnance of sin, it hurts and devalues our relationship with God to a base state.

Joel is the son of Pethuel, but is not placed chronologically by his writing. This book reminds the reader that God will judge and that His justice is perfect. Right relationship with God is to be prized and walking independently with no concern for God's law and righteousness leads to destruction.

Amos saw things concerning Israel in the days of Uzziah the king of Judah, and Jeroboam, the son of Joash, the king of Israel. Amos' writings give us a stark warning to not forget all the things God has blessed us with and to respond by caring for the poor and downtrodden. Treachery, acting to stifle compassion, greed and immorality are strongly condemned and the Lord promises justice in response to these transgressions. The book ends with a promise of restoration.

Obadiah is not chronologically placed by his writings. He wrote a warning to the peoples of Edom (Esau's descendants). He told them to avoid the temptation to take advantage of the Israelites in the day of their judgement. He specifically warned against violence, gloating over their destruction, looting, imprisoning survivors and attacking stragglers.

Jonah was the son of Amittai, he is seen in 2 Kings 14:25. He prophesied for the Israelites during the time of Jeroboam II. He was also called by God to be a messenger to the people of Nineveh, but he was delayed when he sought to sail away in disobedience to his call. He was swallowed by a large fish. Jonah prayed from the belly of the fish. This episode shows that God can use big or little events to turn our hearts towards Him. After three days in the fish he made his way to Nineveh and delivered the message.

There are two main overarching themes to the book; the first is that God is unperturbed and unfettered in the face of human rebellion. God will still accomplish all that He sets out to do. The second major theme is that God is looking over the surface of the whole earth for those who earnestly seek Him. God was concerned about the people and animals of Nineveh even when Jonah was not interested in helping those people. God is not impotent to save men, not in the time of Nineveh, not in the time of Jesus on earth as a physical man and not in contemporary society. God still regards the people of the earth and draws those whom He sees fit to Himself. It would be wrong to lose sight of God's power to soften the human heart.

Micah received his word during the time of the kings Jotham, Ahaz and Hezekiah. Micah's writings remind us that the Lord God is not blind to injustice and evil and He will bring all to account. In the sixth chapter of these writings the people of Israel are reminded of the leadership of Moses, Aaron and Miriam who helped the people start in the right way. It calls the simple ritual worship inadequate because God wants His people to do justice, to love mercy, kindness and to walk humbly with Him. This is incredible by any standard, 'How is it that the Creator of the universe wants something to do with the created beings who are so faulted and minor in scale?' Jesus repeats this theme in Matthew chapter 11 where He says, 'Take my yoke upon you and learn from Me, for I am gentle, humble and you will find rest for your souls.' Micah ends with the promise that we can watch expectantly for the Lord to execute justice, He will bring those who look to Him out of darkness and into the light.

Nahum talked of Nineveh. Nahum, Habakkuk, Zephaniah and Obadiah are thought by scholars to belong to the Neo-Babylonian period (Hill & Walton, p. 463). The writings of Nahum contain a strong warning of the Lord God's power and that He will not leave the guilty unpunished. The Lord is slow to anger and great in power (chapter 1, verse 3).

Habakkuk refers to abuses at the end of the kingdom of Judah. God will use the Chaldeans to seize and punish. The writings warn against idolatry and the evil of violence and bloodshed. Chapter 2 verse 14 of Habakkuk proclaims that the whole earth will be filled with the knowledge of God and the glory of God will cover the earth like the seas. The book ends with a beautiful Psalm that we can all echo, even if things are not going well we know that God is the source of salvation, provides strength and gives us the ability to walk in high places.

Zephaniah writes during the time of Josiah. The Lord will destroy all idol worship, He will restore the remnant of His faithful people, He will devour all evil by the fire of His zeal. He will give purified lips to the people and enable them to serve shoulder to shoulder, from as far as beyond the rivers of Ethiopia, He will gather His people and restore their fortunes.

Haggai writes during the time of the exile. Haggai the prophet speaks to Zerubbabel during the time of rebuilding the Temple in Jerusalem. Although there had been a good start in this work, they faltered when they met opposition. The concentrated on resettling the land upon their return from exile and in so doing left the rebuilding of the Temple as a lost priority. Haggai speaks to the people and their leaders to encourage them, to exhort and confront them to restart the work and to complete the Temple. Haggai and Zechariah are mentioned in Ezra chapter 6. Joel, Haggai,

Zechariah and Malachi are thought to belong to the Persian period of Biblical literature (Hill &

Walton, p. 463). <u>Zechariah</u> also writes during the time of the exile. <u>Malachi</u> is not chronologically

marked by his writings.

Reading from the Bible

    Ezekiel, Daniel, Esther, Ezra, Nehemiah, Haggai, Zechariah, Joel, Malachi.

Congratulations! At this point you have read through the entire Old Testament.

Chapter 6: The Genealogy of Jesus

The Genealogy of Jesus starts the New Testament. Jesus was hailed as the Messiah, this term means anointed savior, and in the Greek language this was the word Christ. Jesus was the descendant of David, the descendant of Abraham. In Matthew 1:1 and following it tells us:

```
Abraham
 |
Isaac
 |
Jacob
 |
Judah-Tamar
 |
Perez
 |
Hezron
 |
Ram
 |
Amminadab
 |
Nahshon
 |
Salmon-Rahab
 |
Boaz-Ruth
 |
Obed
 |
Jesse
 |
David (this is King David)
 |
Solomon
 |
Rehoboam (son of Solomon, he was King during the split of the Kingdom of Israel)
 |
Abijah
 |
Asa
 |
Jehoshaphat
 |
```

```
Joram
 |
Uzziah
 |
Jotham
 |
Ahaz
 |
Hezekiah
 |
Manasseh
 |
Amon
 |
Josiah
 |
Jeconiah (it was around this time that the exile began)
 |
Shealtiel
 |
Zerubbabel
 |
Abiud
 |
Eliakim
 |
Azor
 |
Zadok
 |
Achim
 |
Eliud
 |
Eleazar
 |
Matthan
 |
Jacob
 |
Joseph (the husband of Mary)
 |
Jesus (called Christ)
```

Through Jesus all people can become heirs of Abraham (see John 1:12 and Galatians 4:4-6). In

Luke 3:23-38, it gives an additional list of ancestors:

```
Adam (son of God)
 |
Seth
 |
Enosh
 |
Cainan
 |
Mahalaleel
 |
Jared
 |
Enoch
 |
Methuselah
 |
Lamech
 |
Noah (built the ark)
 |
Shem
 |
Arphaxad
 |
Cainan
 |
Shelah
 |
Heber
 |
Peleg
 |
Reu
 |
Serug
 |
Nahor
 |
Terah
 |
Abraham (son of Terah)
 |
```

Isaac (Isaac was the father of twins: Jacob and Esau)
 |
Jacob
 |
Judah
 |
Perez
 |
Hezron
 |
Ram
 |
Admin
 |
Amminadab
 |
Nahshon
 |
Salmon
 |
Boaz
 |
Obed
 |
Jesse
 |
David (became king, was the son of Jesse and father of King Solomon)
 |
Nathan
 |
Mattatha
 |
Menna
 |
Melea
 |
Eliakim
 |
Jonam
 |
Joseph
 |
Judah
 |
Simeon
 |

Levi
|
Matthat
|
Jorim
|
Eliezer
|
Joshua
|
Er
|
Elmadam
|
Cosam
|
Addi
|
Melchi
|
Neri
|
Shealtiel
|
Zerubbabel
|
Rhesa
|
Joanan
|
Joda
|
Josech
|
Semein
|
Mattathias
|
Maath
|
Naggai
|
Hesli
|
Nahum
|

```
Amos
 |
Mattathias
 |
Joseph
 |
Jannai
 |
Melchi
 |
Levi
 |
Matthat
 |
Eli
 |
Joseph
 |
Jesus (supposedly the earthly son of Joseph, the Son of God).
```

The New Testament Structure

The New Testament is composed of books written about Jesus and His followers. It starts

with four accounts of Jesus' life, work, ministry, miracles, death and resurrection. These four are

called the Gospels. After the gospel accounts of Jesus, we have a series of writings by apostles

(those appointed by Jesus to serve in His ministry) and teachers that complete the canon

(recognized collection of Scripture). The form of some of these writings is that of an ancient letter.

Some of these writers include, Peter, Paul (who met Jesus on the way to Damascus), John, Jude,

James, Luke, Mark and Matthew.

The Gospels

There are four parallel Gospel accounts, these accounts record the life and work of Jesus.

Mark is thought to be the earliest account of Jesus' life and ministry. Matthew and Luke were

likely written after Mark. The last gospel account to be written was John. It was written by the

Apostle John who is thought to have lived the longest and to have written his account the latest.

The book of <u>Acts</u> was written by a man named Luke. He was a companion of the Apostle Paul and a physician. He also wrote the gospel of <u>Luke</u>. The two books form a detailed description of Jesus' life, followed by the story of the growth of the belief in Jesus as the Savior. Luke and Acts form a two volume set by one writer in this sense. Acts covers a period of several years, up to a point about 35 years after Christ's death and resurrection. Luke was a traveling companion and help to the Apostle Paul.

The Letters

There are two groupings of letters, there are those written by Paul and then there are those penned by other writers. Paul's dramatic conversion is recorded in Acts 9. Paul then travelled and ministered throughout the Mediterranean basin. There were numerous responses to the teachings about Jesus, and as groups of Christians started forming Paul would write to them. His letters carry instruction, warning and direction for the growing communities and it is these letters that are preserved.

Paul wrote a letter to the <u>Romans,</u> this is an interesting letter clearly laying out his positions since he has not met most of them in person. Paul also writes to the church in Corinth and this is preserved as the two letters to them, <u>1 Corinthians</u> and <u>2 Corinthians</u>. Paul's earliest letter is thought to be <u>Galatians,</u> written to a church in the territory that is found in modern day Turkey. <u>1 Thessalonians</u> and <u>2 Thessalonians</u> are also thought to be written by Paul early on in his ministry. <u>Ephesians,</u> <u>Philippians</u> and <u>Colossians</u> are all written to groups of believers by Paul, these groups are located geographically in places that are in modern day Greece and Turkey. Paul also wrote to two of his delegates, a younger man and partner in ministry named Timothy, and another named

Titus. These letters are 1 Timothy, 2 Timothy and Titus. Paul also writes a letter to a man named

Philemon.

The second group of letters is sometimes called the general epistles. James was written by

James an early leader in the Church and was likely written earliest of all the books in the New

Testament. It fits with the timing described in the book of Acts, in chapter 8. The book of Hebrews

is sometimes attributed to the Apostle Paul but the author is unknown. 1 Peter and 2 Peter were

written by Jesus' close companion, the Apostle Peter. These letters confirm Paul's writings (see 2

Peter 3:15-16) and reassure believers about the timing of the second coming of Jesus.

The Apostle John wrote the gospel account of Jesus' life called John. John also wrote

additional letters. John's three letters are 1 John, 2 John and 3 John. The vision John received also

was penned in the style of a letter, and called Revelation. Jude is a short book that has many

parallels to 2 Peter and gives a wonderful picture of the believer's station. He encourages the

reader by stating that God 'is able to keep you from stumbling, and to make you stand in the

presence of His glory blameless with great joy.'

The New Testament as it is called, describes the rise of Christianity from it's Jewish origins

and the life and ministry of Jesus. The authors explain their own beliefs in Jesus as the Chosen

One. Jesus was the predicted sin solution for all time; He healed the rupture between God and

humankind. He accomplished what no previous system or religion could accomplish by purifying a

people for Himself made up of those who call on Him and believe in His saving sacrifice. He did

this by making a sacrifice for sins. He offered Himself as that sacrifice and this act covered all sin

and error. By covering sin and satisfying God's justice, Jesus created a path to God. All humans

have the opportunity irrespective of background to walk that path to redemption and renewal. This was made possible because Jesus paid the price for sin when He died on the cross. He lived a perfect life, He was killed, buried and on the third day He rose from the dead. The New Testament goes on to explain that Jesus is now stationed in heaven where He is the one mediator between God and humankind.

Reading from the Bible

A suggested reading of the New Testament would look like this,

Mark, Luke, Acts chapters 1-8,

James, Acts chapters 9-15, Galatians,

Acts chapters 16-28,

1 Thessalonians, 2 Thessalonians,

1 Corinthians, 2 Corinthians,

Romans,

Ephesians, Colossians, Phillipians,

Philemon,

Matthew,

1 Timothy, 2 Timothy, Titus,

John,

Hebrews,

1 Peter, 2 Peter, Jude,

1 John, 2 John, 3 John,

Revelation.

Congratulations! You have read the entire book.

There are several ways to interact with the text, most simply by asking questions. Perhaps some of the following questions have been answered, fill in your own notes and references next to the questions.

Are we all one family? Colossians 3:11, _____

Does the Bible make sense? 1 Corinthians 1:23, 1 Corinthians 2:14, _____

Who are all the people in the Bible? Revelation 20:12-13, Romans 10:12, _____

Is it believable or make believe? Romans 10:9, _____ _____

Is God accessible? Romans 10:13, _____

Does God have a plan for creation? Jeremiah 29:11-12, _____ _____

Does this plan include me? John 3:16, _____

Who was Jesus? Why did he have to die? Is the Bible relevant to modern life? _____

What is gained from reading the Bible? Isaiah 55:6-11, Luke 9:23-26, _____

Why is prayer and asking for Holy Spirit's guidance so important? I Corinthians 2:14, _____

What did you appreciate most in the readings? _____

What didn't you like or find helpful? _____

What did you learn about God? _____

What response do you have? What do you need to do in response? _____

What are you hoping in? What are you hoping for? _____

What do you plan on doing going forward? _____

Conclusion

There is much more that could be written here and has been already written elsewhere to encourage and to purposefully press people to read the Bible. The reading of the Holy Scriptures has not continued at the pace one would expect for such an esteemed and ancient text. The text is recognized by Christians and Jews. The selections called the Law, the Zabur of David and the Gospels are also recognized by followers of the Islamic faith. A broad part of the modern world is populated by people that hold these beliefs dear. Another large part of the world is influenced by these beliefs. The followers of many traditions would hold that these accounts are useful. Considering this wide spread influence, the reading of the texts should be more robust. There should be more fruitful discussion and interaction across the spectrum of age, ethnicity and social status to interact with these writings. We can surmise that there is much to be gleaned from intentional and specific readings in these substantive areas.

One can read further literature and by searching additional books can find much aid with the context and the cultural background of the texts. There are excellent commentaries that help explain what is read, in particular the works of D.A. Carson, John MacArthur and other scholars are well esteemed. There are numerous books to give further guidance to the reading of these Holy Scriptures. This book can be the first step in that lifelong pursuit. The attention must be focused however on the source and the backbone of all the commentaries, that means taking a closer look at the words contained in the Holy Scriptures themselves.

Perhaps for some all this can seem cumbersome, perhaps overbearing or impossible; it seems overwhelming to sit down and read the whole Bible or even one book in the Bible. The suggestion here is to start by reading three chapters a day and see where it takes you. Start a book club in your home among family members and friends. The group can compare notes, compile questions and enjoy the process of reading through together. In today's age, it can be done online in a social media facilitated conversation and beyond. There are also numerous online tools such as www.blueletterbible.org that can aid and contribute to the reader's understanding. The ultimate source of the return on time invested in the Scriptures however comes from the Lord, a faith in Him and His doings in the world. In the 55th chapter of Isaiah, it is stated as follows,

> 6 Seek the LORD while He may be found;
> Call upon Him while He is near.
> 7 Let the wicked forsake his way
> And the unrighteous man his thoughts;
> And let him return to the LORD,
> And He will have compassion on him,
> And to our God,
> For He will abundantly pardon.
> 8 "For My thoughts are not your thoughts,
> Nor are your ways My ways," declares the LORD.
> 9 "For *as* the heavens are higher than the earth,
> So are My ways higher than your ways
> And My thoughts than your thoughts.
> 10 "For as the rain and the snow come down from heaven,
> And do not return there without watering the earth
> And making it bear and sprout,
> And furnishing seed to the sower and bread to the eater;
> 11 So will My word be which goes forth from My mouth;
> It will not return to Me empty,
> Without accomplishing what I desire,
> And without succeeding *in the matter* for which I sent it.

There is a return on the time investment, in searching and reading the Scriptures, it is not a fruitless activity. It does not return empty.

Enjoy your read and Many blessings!

References

Costecalde, C. Editor, & Dennis, P. (1997). <u>Family Bible.</u> New York, NY: DK Publishing.

Gundry, R.H. (2003). <u>A Survey of the New Testament</u> 4th Edition. Grand Rapids, MI: Zondervan.

Hill, A. E., & Walton, J.H. (2000). <u>A Survey of the Old Testament</u> 2nd Edition. Grand Rapids, MI:

Zondervan.

Walton, J.H. (1994). <u>Chronological and Background Charts of the Old Testament</u>. Grand Rapids,

MI: Zondervan.

<u>New American Standard Bible Reference Edition</u> (1977). Chicago, Il: Moody Press.